MUST DO BEFORE YOU DIE

LEARN, APPLY, RECORD AND SHARE

NIRAJ KUMAR SINGH

Copyright © Niraj Kumar Singh
All Rights Reserved.

This book has been published with all efforts taken to make the material error-free after the consent of the author. However, the author and the publisher do not assume and hereby disclaim any liability to any party for any loss, damage, or disruption caused by errors or omissions, whether such errors or omissions result from negligence, accident, or any other cause.

While every effort has been made to avoid any mistake or omission, this publication is being sold on the condition and understanding that neither the author nor the publishers or printers would be liable in any manner to any person by reason of any mistake or omission in this publication or for any action taken or omitted to be taken or advice rendered or accepted on the basis of this work. For any defect in printing or binding the publishers will be liable only to replace the defective copy by another copy of this work then available.

To my wife (Nilotpala Sarma) and our Son Rushank Kumar Singh. Without your unwavering support, sacrifice, and belief in me, this work would not be possible.

Contents

"Knowledge is power: You hear it all the time but knowledge is not power. It's only potential power. It only becomes power when we apply it and use it.

Somebody who reads a book and doesn't apply it they're at no advantage over someone who's illiterate.

None of it works unless YOU work. We have to do our part. If knowing is half the battle, action is the second half of the battle."
— Jim Kwik

CHAPTER ONE

INTRODUCTION

Over the past few years, video content has exploded in popularity across the globe. You see videos everywhere – on television, social media, text messages, billboards, online advertisements, and even on restaurant menus.

Because videos have become so prominent among the rising generation, creating videos of your own has become easier.

Today, everyone has instant access to filming, editing and publishing videos.This way videos have started a revolution in offering us the convenience of easy information that can be quickly grasped.

And in case you are unaware about the huge impact and importance of video content for your own growth personally and financially , then I encourage you to read this Book.

This Book aims to give you a strong reason for creating videos immediately. Also you will learn about growing exponentially in multifarious ways by making videos.

If you do this strategically it will really help you achieve your most valued aspirations in life. Eventually, this book also enables you to understand the techniques of video creation.

With that aim in mind, this Book is divided into two key parts: the first is the mindset part and second is skillset part.

Perhaps for the newbie, this may be a bit of an awakening, but the fact is that there are a variety of videos that enable different objectives.

For instance if entertainment is the objective then,you can create music videos, if you are good at singing and playing some instruments.

Or you can make funny videos about jokes, pranks, comedy, etc.

You can make videos to share whatever you're doing or planning to achieve.

But here,I am not talking about entertainment only.

I'm talking about extremely valuable content.

I am talking about videos where you share your ideas, values, thoughts, suggestions, or maybe something which is related to your work.

What do I mean by that?

Well,consider this; it's like you're at work in your office and learning something very significant.

And you feel obligated to share your learning with others. Hence you proceed to share your learning online.

Now when you do that you build a relationship which is critical for you and your online counterparts.

That's because even though you are not meeting people one on one, you share something significant which adds value and helps other people to grow in their life.

But the interesting thing is that by adding value to others you also add value to yourself.

Your self esteem rises, your confidence increases in yourself, and your overall outlook toward life becomes positive.

So you see, how easy and fast it helps you to grow in your life and relationship.

Also, please note when I talk about non entertainment videos I mean, crucial life transforming, value enhancing content..

For example, you know some very interesting techniques which can help people to finish some task within three hours, which would otherwise have taken five hours.

This kind of knowledge, when shared through video content, makes a deep impact on peoples' lives.

Say you are an expert at PowerPoint Presentation, in this case then you could share your skills with people and enable them to grow in their careers to achieve what they wanted to achieve.

I am talking about such kinds of videos because it is the only way to motivate and inspire people very fast.

It doesn't matter where you are in life,but what's important is that if you possess some unique information then make it a point to spread that knowledge around you.

And when you share your ideas through video content, you add value and also educate, influence and inspire.

MINDSET

CHAPTER TWO

ARE WE SAYING NO TO VIDEO?

Imagine for a moment, while going through this Book you may suddenly say, "Niraj I am not very keen on making videos".

If that's the case I respect your views.

But could you just stand back and look at this from a different perspective?

Well, here's the thing.

When you say no to making videos fundamentally you are saying no to the best affordable resources at this point of time to grow in your life.

To understand that, let me correlate with the theory of evolution.

If you see the evolution of human beings, the only reason we are at the peak of evolution is because of a crucial facet.

You may ask me what I mean by the peak of evolution?

Well, the fact is that the human body and the brain are the most evolved body and brain on this planet. That's the reason we have this vivid imagination, and we have this extremely developed memory.

The kind of imagination and memory we have, very few animals possess the same.

The truth is that these attributes help us to stay on top of things on this planet.

But this has happened over a long period of time by adapting to our environment and by saying gradually yes to adapting and working with available resources.

When you say no to videos, you are not just saying no to technology, you are not just saying no to speaking in front of the camera, but you are saying no to the best resource available in your life.

Look around, and you just go back to the evolution; we have reached where we are today only because our ancestors used the best resources available.

If you are among those people who say, OK, Niraj, I will think about whether I should make videos or not. Indirectly saying that, ok Niraj, I will think about it.

But.

The best resources available right now,

The best option available right now,

The best opportunity in front of you right now to grow in your life is with you.

And you are saying, Niraj, I will think about it!

So essentially, what am I saying?

Here's what I'm saying.

You are aware of current resources and craft at this point. Videos are one of the best sources of increasing your business. Use videos to share your ideas, and thoughts with people and grow in your life.

CHAPTER THREE

I AM TOO BUSY, I DON'T HAVE TIME TO MAKE VIDEOS

One of the significant reasons why people don't make videos is that they are busy.

But I ask, what if you are busy in your professional life? There is only one goal: to grow in your life, isn't it?

Here's a possible scenario.

Imagine you are busy in sales because you want to grow in sales.

You want to become a national sales manager or maybe more significant than that.

Right?

But what if your profession is like a doctor, lawyer, or sales Manager?

Doubtlessly, you'll also be equally busy trying to grow in that field.

So you see, you are busy because you want to grow in that area.

Eventually, if you are a busy professional, it means the only reason to stay engaged is that you want to grow.

If you recollect, I mentioned at the outset that we only want to make videos for one reason - to grow in our life.

But here's an interesting point.

A busy person is ideal for creating videos.

If you are too busy, then you are in a better position to make videos.

Why?

Because the documented fact is that you invariably learn more than others when you work hard, and this also means you have great content to share with the world.

So what's the advantage of that?

Consider this.

Suppose you are in sales, and you decide to make a 5-minute video about your learning in sales every week, and you upload a video series on LinkedIn, your Facebook Page or your YouTube channel. You'll be pleasantly surprised to note that merely adding videos in small instalments will inevitably add to a massive YouTube channel. That's how most YouTubers gain success.

Now please note the significant part. Here, I am asking you to upload only one video every week.

But when you do this for a significant period and if you record more than 15 to 20 videos, do you know what will happen?

You'll have a compelling presence online that will speak volumes about your ability all over the internet.

And this is a massive strength for gaining new businesses or even a job.

How?

Let me clarify with an example.

You are a sales guy, and you have an upcoming interview. But even before the interview, your employers access your videos highlighting your idea or message on sales. (Remember, sales is your passion).

Won't they be more impressed with your commitment toward sales compared to any other candidate without supporting video content?

Why do I give this example about a job interview?

Because nowadays, many recruiters routinely check candidates' social media profiles before the interview. And in case they do have a social media presence or video content, what do you think will happen?

Here, you have 50% better chances of landing a job as your videos prove your ability and commitment to sales.

No wonder today so many successful professionals- doctors, lawyers, and architects, despite their busy schedules- frequently create and post 4-to-5-minute videos on social media channels like youtube, Instagram, LinkedIn and many more channels.

And when you do that, you are telling the world that you are different from others because you believe in learning at the same time and sharing that with the world.

Before going to the next chapter, pause and ask yourself, "if all busy professionals can make videos, why can't you?"

CHAPTER FOUR

IGNORE THE 1%, FOCUS ON 99%

The most common reason why people do not make videos is that they feel what others will think.

What will someone say?

I remember for the first time when I uploaded my first video. I got the 1st comment; you know what? It was "Ver Funny."

Then, it was very painful for me.

Painful because I had no idea what intention he wrote that comment. I was expecting some good comments and some good feedback.

I shared my ideas, thoughts, whatever, but many people don't make videos and share their learnings because they feel that people do not react well if they make videos.

If people do not give good comments or feedback, they will feel bad about it.

No matter who you are?

Where are you in your life?

When you make a video, at least one person will criticise you and put you down by giving nasty comments or feedback.

But unfortunately, not everyone is that good at communicating in front of others. You may have some problems with your language or the kinds of words You choose.

Remember this line.

There are two types of people on this planet: 1% people and 99% people. 1% of people will always comment negatively or criticise you in your video-making journey.

Ignore 1% negative people because you still have 99% good people who will always inspire and motivate you in your journey.

If you upload your video on Facebook, YouTube or LinkedIn, you may reach millions of people every week. If I calculate numbers, only 1% of people react with anger and nasty comments on your video, but 99% of people will still like your videos. This 99% of people will give good feedback even if they don't like it.

If only that 1% of people are stopping you from making videos, then,

I must tell you; you will find these kinds of 1% people everywhere in your life, In every department, in every area of your life and even in your office.

If you do something, you will find that 1% of people will discourage you and not like you.

And if those 1% people are stopping you from creating videos, then you are doing injustice with you, with your content and at the same time, you are doing injustice to your 99% people who want to listen to you, to your ideas, thoughts and beliefs.

And it's your social responsibility to respect that positive 99 % of people.

So, Please ignore the 1%, and focus on 99%.

CHAPTER FIVE

MAKE A VIDEO TO STAY HAPPY

Let's understand that making videos are related to growth, not just talking about financial gain.

Many times, people believe that you will learn how to make videos, and you start one YouTube channel and then monetise that channel and earn a lot of money.

If your idea of making videos is only that, then you are losing your opportunity.

Let's understand how videos are related to growth and the happiness of your life.

An American Psychiatrist, Robert Waldinger was the study director of a study that Harvard University was doing for 75 years and is the longest study done by any university on humankind.

Yes, what you mean by that,

They tracked the lives of hundreds of people for 75 years, from a very early age to the last few years of life.

They track the life of hundreds of people related to their- bank balance, financial stability, health records, career records, social life and so on.

Why does Harvard University do this? Which is the longest study on humans to find the answer to only one question: what makes human beings happy?

"The surprising finding is that our relationships and how happy we are in our relationships have a powerful influence on our health," said Robert Waldinger,

Director of the study, a psychiatrist at Massachusetts General Hospital and a professor of psychiatry at Harvard Medical School. "Taking care of your body is important, but tending to your relationships is a form of self-care too. That, I think, is the revelation." (Source news.harvard.edu)

The study revealed that close relationships, more than money or fame, keep people happy.

So, those with healthy and good relationships are happy and live even 15 or 16 years more than other unhappy people.

So, Whenever you want to build a relationship, you give imaginary sharing like your pencil or your chocolate with someone just because you like that person; you want to double your relationship.

And you know that if you give something to that person, he will also give something to you.

You will again give back something not necessarily tangible. Sometimes just ideas, hot stories for spending time together.

When you share something, you build a relationship. And if you are making videos and sharing your values, skills, and thoughts, which you are giving to the world, you are making relationships with them.

A lot of people want to live with themselves only. They don't want people in their life.

But I have seen some people who are not very happy because they don't have people in their life.

When you have people in your life, you get opportunities, and the opportunity will never come from the cloud; it will come from people only.

Whether you believe in God or don't believe in God is a separate issue, but you need people. And I think that God will use people as a vehicle to give opportunities to you.

And when you have more people, you will get more opportunities, and as a result, you can make more relationships with them.

You get more relationships and grow in your life when you make videos and share your ideas, values, and thoughts with people.

And when you make regular videos, you are using the best technology available right now to help you disseminate your knowledge, new ideas, and thoughts.

And when you make relationships, you stay happy in your life.

So, make videos to stay happy and grow in your life.

CHAPTER SIX

MAKE VIDEOS TO BUILD A SOCIAL IMAGE

The most important topic, which will change your life if you make videos seriously in your career.

As many as 70 per cent of employers these days go through a candidate's social media profile before hiring them.

Even in business, investors check the social media profile of a founder's directors to see what exactly there is on social media.

Let me share my real experience with social media. I remember 5 years back My principal told me that she was going to take an interview for the post of teacher and later asked me to check the candidate's social media profile and submit the report. The exciting thing is that it was a private school, not any MNC or Private Company.

Suppose you are in sales and you have good experience of sales. Then make video series and upload them on social media profiles. This will give you extra weightage at the time of the interview or any recruitment.

If you are in marketing, then make videos on marketing.

No matter your business, making videos on your product and company will give you some extra benefits to your career.

When the HR recruiter notices your video, it's giving a message, creating an image that you are a well-experienced person and doing it effectively. That image is beneficial for living in the world.

Nowadays, social media will decide your image before you meet your life partner.

So, take the video seriously on your topic or skill. It can help you to grow in your job or your business.

CHAPTER SEVEN

My Content is Not Worth Sharing

One very common reason why people do not make videos is that they feel they don't have that content that is worth sharing with the world.

Many people think that it's too early for them to share the content among people.

Look around between offices. Those people were in their 40s and 50's years; how many shared the content on social media?

Maybe No one.

As per the study, only 20% of people develop content, and around 80% of people just consume the content created by 20%.

See how many people are sitting around you in your office?

How many are creating content on social media?

How many people are creating content, writing articles, and making videos around you in your office?

Most of them are consuming content, not creating anything on social media.

How long will you just read others' books?

How long will you just read others' quotes?

How long will you just watch others' videos?

Some people say that they don't have to do this.

Please don't say you don't have to do this.

You have to do this as you love to read books and watch videos, and for how long will you just be that 80%?

When you will come in the 20%. No matter where you are in your life. The people just below you are looking towards you and want you to tell them how you have reached there.

At the same time, people are looking at you and expecting from your content, ideas, values and so on.

Let me give you one example.

There are three types of people

1. Top-level people: These people create content.

2. Middle-Level People: It's you; consume content from top-level people

3. Lower-Level People: Waiting to consume content from Middle-Level People.

From the above example, I would like to say that you are consuming information/content from the Top Level, but what about the Lower-Level people? They are still waiting for your content.

As a Middle-level person, it's your social responsibility to create content for lower-level people. Because they expect from you, not from top-level people.

So, you always look for people who are above you and there are many things which you have achieved in your life by learning from them.

So, it's your responsibility to tell the world where you have reached, and how you have reached; at the same time, it's your responsibility to look up, find people in your life far better than you learn from them and go towards them.

It's never late; start now; even if this is day 1 in your office, you can still make a video of your day one experience and how you rock the stage.

Like, How they react when you're giving your introduction to people and what are the do's and don'ts of the one in your office.

Many people want to know what they should do when they join the office on day one.

Yes, there is an audience for every piece of content, but unfortunately, only 20% of people create content and the remaining 80% consume content.

The time has come when you have to shift from 80% to 20% and making a video is the most effective way of creating content. You just need a smartphone.

Nowadays, you have all the resources; you just need to make a video, and for that, only one thing is required, i.e. change in mindset alarm to come from this 80% to 20%.

Just you have to change your mindset and tell yourself that

Yes, I will read books and articles, and at the same time, I will write and make videos about what I have learned.

I will shift myself from 80% to 20%.

I will create videos to grow in my life.

CHAPTER EIGHT

WHAT IF I AM CAMERA SHY

One question that might be disturbing you or appearing in your mind is that Niraj, I am not very good in front of the camera.

I don't speak effectively in front of the camera, and I am unable to engage the audience in front of the camera, I have never spoken in front of the camera.

But when you made the video, you found it was not impressive, maybe because of that.

If you still think that you are not interested in making videos, understand one very simple thing like any other skill; even making videos is a simple skill.

The easiest way to understand this is by taking the example of bike riding on day 1.

When you start riding a bike as a new member for the first time, you may be scared about all bike mechanisms like brakes, clutch, accelerator, gear etc., but later, you master it by riding regularly.

You master it because you started learning this like any other skill.

Now, you are riding a bike naturally because you learnt the skill of riding.

You can even raise one hand to say bye to your family member while riding a bike.

For driving a car, some people hire mentors to learn the skill. On day 1, you cannot go smoothly, and it will take time to master the driving skills.

In the same way, you have to learn the skills of making videos and facing cameras.

If you expect that without learning this skill, you will go in front of the camera and make a viral video, but nothing will happen like that.

Now again, You may be telling....

Niraj, I don't want to make videos because I am not good at the camera.

I am not, I don't look good on camera.

I don't know how to speak on camera but remember, only babies are born on this planet.

If you see the old videos of famous people, you will find the same thing happening inside you; you can even ask them to share their first video.

Good people will always love to share and not hesitate to share what they have done and how it was.

They will tell you that it was poor, lacking confidence. Because every time whenever we do something for the first time it's always something like this only.

I am looking for that first attempt only if you are doing that. It's just like you joining swimming class today.

On the day of joining the swimming class, you do not learn even one or two lessons about swimming. And you're expecting you to swim smoothly from day one, but it's impossible, my friends.

Here the same conditions are applied while making videos like any other skill. You have to learn it.

My friends, please stay away from these words like - I don't look good on videos, I am not very comfortable in front of the camera, I am a camera-shy person,

Please come on and learn the techniques but first, accept that you're expecting to make good videos without knowing the skill.

It is as good as you're expecting, swimming inside the water without learning how to swim. That is not possible.

Please stop thinking that you are not good in front of the camera. First, you try, then blame yourself.

CHAPTER NINE

WHY I SHOULD SHARE MY CONTENTS?

Sometimes people do not make videos for this simple reason;

They think this is my idea, thoughts, suggestions, content, and why I should share it with the world.

Imagine this.

If you think like this,

then just imagine this simple scenario.

You are heading a Software IT Company. And You have one vacancy in your team.

Two candidates are sitting outside, and you have to choose one.

The vacancy is for a software engineer.

The first person comes inside, and you evaluate that the person has all the skills required to develop software.

But during the conversation, you observe that this person is very introverted and unable to speak effectively. This person clearly says he dislikes talking in front of people.

After the deep conversation, you come to know that in the entire previous journey never spoken in front of people.

The second person comes inside, and you evaluate that person and find all the required skills to develop software. But you noticed that the second person has good communication skills. He wants to share his learning with the world.

He loves to communicate with people.

Even he is sharing his learning and mistakes with the world on social platforms.

Now you tell me whom you select for the vacancy.

1st Candidate - Have all required skills to develop software, very introverted, does not like to speak with people and is unable to communicate effectively.

2nd Candidate- Have all required skills to develop software, good communication skills, love to work in a team, sharing his ideas, values and thoughts with people.

I know you have selected the second candidate because of his other soft skills.

People who love to share ideas, thoughts, learning and mistakes grow very fast in life.

Make videos and strengthen your habit of sharing with the world.

SKILLSET

CHAPTER TEN

EQUIPMENT TO MAKE VIDEOS.

You need some essential equipment for making good engagement videos, and here I'm not talking about investing in expensive DSLR Cameras, audio systems, lighting systems and tripods.

At the start, you just don't have to invest too much money in this equipment.

Your primary goal is to make basic Videos.

It will help you double your relationship and share your ideas, values and thoughts with the people.

The four basic requirements are enough for making basic videos.

The first is your recording device; no need to buy a DSLR Camera, your smartphone is enough to record any video, and it's always with you.

Here you don't have to do any setup like DSLR Cameras.

Now, you don't say that you don't have a good smartphone. If you don't have a good smartphone, just get it.

I have noticed that the price of the new model smartphone is not very high, and they focus more on the camera and quality of the camera.

So, you will get the best smartphone with the best camera by paying Rs.10,000.00

Source - Pixabay.com

This small investment should not stop you from making videos. Start making videos with your smartphone. Smartphones are enough to make videos.

CHAPTER ELEVEN

NEXT IS AUDIO

Another tool required to make good videos is good audio quality.

See, no matter how good you look on video, if your Audio is not clear and has too much background noise, it is disturbing for your audience.

I suggest you invest around 900 to 1200 rupees on Boya mic (BY M1). You will get it on amazon.

Boya Mic Features: -

· Boya BYM1 Omnidirectional Lavalier Condenser Microphone with 20ft Audio Cable (Black)

· EASY TO CLIP No hassle to clip it. Just clip the MIC on your outfit and start recording your voice.

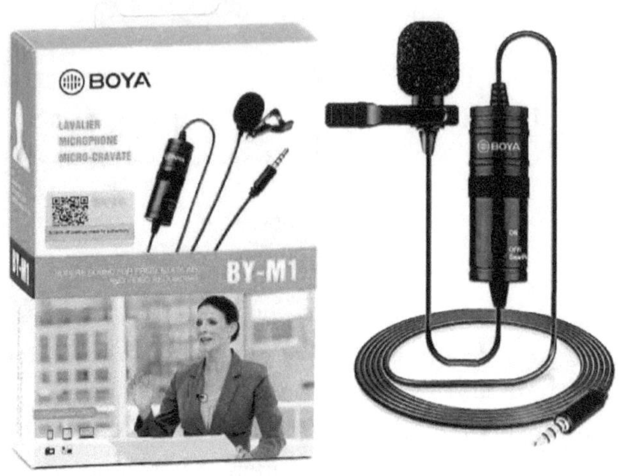

Source - Google

You can use your mic, which is available with you.

Note: - If you face any problem while recording Audio on your smartphone, you can install an open camera application from Play Store. This application will help you to record videos with Audio. Even You can search on YouTube for "how to connect Boya mic with open Camera."

CHAPTER TWELVE

HOW DO I FIND MY TRUE PASSION

It is an essential part of the video-making journey. You might have a question about how to choose your passion.

Or how can you know that sales are your passion,

how can you know that giving value is your passion,

how can you know that public speaking is your passion,

how can you know that helping people is your passion?

We know that you have come to know that sales are your passion or that Digital Marketing is your passion.

To know your passion, you have to think about your day-to-day life.

When people come to you and why?

People proactively come to you and ask for your help in that niche.

For example, digital marketing people coming to you and asking for help,

salespeople coming to you and asking for help,

marketing people coming to you and asking for help,

your colleague coming to you and asking for help on excel, tally or on any different financial products like Insurance, PPF, Income Tax, etc.

Self-declaration is not going to help people;

you have to do it. Yes if you are doing good in something like sales or anything, people will observe that you are doing good, you are getting good results, and people want to replicate those results.

If people come to you again and again for your knowledge, not only people from your own family but people from various parts, from office colleagues and friends, it means that you can share that knowledge with more people by making videos.

But if you don't have those types of people, then don't worry still you can make non-specific video series but start under one campaign; maybe the most straightforward way here is "learning of your life", it's easy, to begin with.

But remember, do not make meaningless videos.

Try to give a value which will change the life of viewers.

Sharing one video every week will be enough but make sure when you are sharing that learning is significant, it helps you in your life.

Don't make videos just for the sake of making a video.

Always choose life-changing topics which will help people to grow in their life after watching your videos.

CHAPTER THIRTEEN

HOW TO FIND THE TOPIC?

No.1 question which you have to answer to make an effective and engaging video is.

The topic on which you are making the video?

Your topic is questionable unless and until you are not talking very passionately about that.

If you are not inspired, you will not be able to inspire others.

So, finding the topic on which you want to make videos is essential.

How to do that?

Here are the ways of doing that.

First, you have to answer if there is anyone topic, one specific topic on which you want to make videos.

An example could be if you are a runner, a half-marathon runner, and you want to teach people how to run for your health-conscious, or you know the techniques and methods of staying fit, you can teach people how to do that.

Suppose you are good in relationships and counselling, and here you can teach people how to maintain that love and how to do counselling.

You can teach people how to make sales if you are good at sales.

You can teach people how to do yoga and stay fit if you are good at Yoga.

If you don't have a specific topic, then just find it because if you don't have any particular topic, how you will make videos, and what topic you will choose.

Don't worry; you can still make videos, you can make random videos but under one campaign/niche.

Listen to this very carefully,

Try to understand that you are making videos for people, not yourself, and you will publish these videos on social media.

You have to understand that the whole idea of making a video is to grow in your life, even if you are creating random videos, but you have to make it under one campaign/niche.

You might be thinking that by making one video, your video will be viral, and you will become famous.

But in reality, it's not like that.

Even if You are super busy, you should record at least one video weekly.

If you are not doing one video per week, it is tough to capture the attention of the social media audience.

At the start, you don't have to work on the thumbnail; you just focus on recording video series (15 to 20 videos of 5 to 7 minutes) because here I am talking about your passion, interest, etc.

CHAPTER FOURTEEN

LIGHTS

Another requirement is lighting, or it may not be required. It all depends on where you are making the video.

If you are recording a video indoors with no natural light, you must need lights because lighting plays a vital role while shooting a video.

If you have enough light in your room, you won't have to invest money in a lighting system, but you can invest a small amount in buying lights to look professional.

You can buy one ring light from Amazon at a discounted price.

As you are new to the video-making journey, do not buy expensive lights.

If you don't have money to invest, you can record videos just near your window but only in the daytime.

You can buy this type of light from amazon. (Investment Rs. 1500 to 2000).

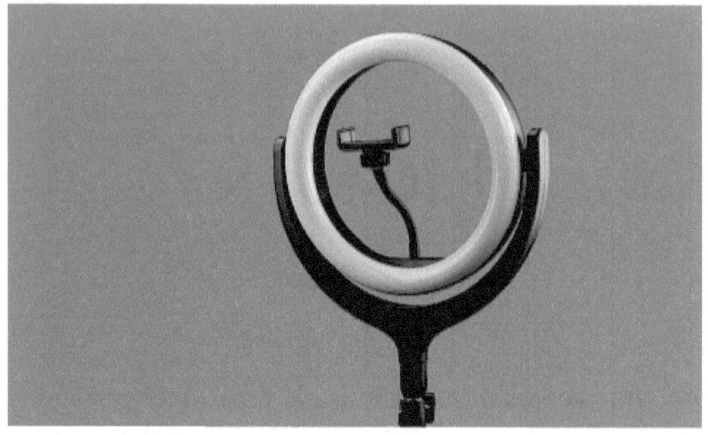

Source - Pixabay

Please check the mobile holder before purchasing.

CHAPTER FIFTEEN

MAKING VIDEO IS A SKILL

Let's understand what the skills required to make videos are.

You expect that you will go in front of the camera, make videos and people like your videos, and become famous.

Please understand what you want to convey without learning a few basic skills of video making.

It is as good as you expect to drive a car without learning to drive.

Both possibilities are not possible, and these are unfair expectations.

Your content helps you to engage your audiences.

Engaging audiences is the best skill when you make any videos.

So, you have to focus on your content to engage the audience.

Sometimes you will feel that you don't have any content to share with the world.

If you feel that you don't have content, you can watch YouTube videos on your topic.

Get ideas from that topic and make your video.

Sometimes you may get content ideas from social media groups.

You can list all questions asked by different group members on your topic and later give solutions in your video.

So, give your best while making a video to engage the audience because engaging the audience is a skill.

You have to master this skill to grow fast.

ORGANIZING YOUR VIDEO CONTENT

I know it's challenging to organize video content, but you can do it easily with the help of some process, and that process is container theory.

The 3 Container Theory: - This is the best way of organising video content on any topic. Let's take the example of "Investment."

Container 1 - Research Google on investment within 120 words.

Container 2 - Get Some quotes from Global Authority on that particular topic. If you are talking about investment then you can give an example of Warren Buffet in your video.

Container 3 - Here, you will share your experience /knowledge on investment.

Let's assume your upcoming video topic is "Where to invest money to become rich."

Then you have to start your video with the following steps.

Step 1: - Start with questions like "Do You know where to invest money to become rich? You can ask more than 3 or more questions.

Step 2: - Here, you have to give an idea about investing money and becoming rich (Search on Google)

Step 3: - Mention quotes by Warren Buffet on investment.

Step 4: - Here, you will share your practical learning or your experience on investment and becoming rich.

Step 5: - End Your Video. (You can end your video by saying anything like "Thank You", or "Bye Bye". it's up to you.)

These are the best 5 steps for organising and creating video content.

CHAPTER SEVENTEEN

TRIPOD

The 4th thing is that you have to invest in a tripod. Like any other tool, you can quickly get a tripod for around Rs.400 to 500 based on your budget.

Even here, you can go up to Rs.5000 to Rs.6000 tripods which is up to you.

But you can start with the lowest priced one.

First, do not invest too much in video-making tools.

It will serve the purpose. While buying a tripod, don't forget to check the mobile holder.

Benefits of Tripod: -

1. You can put this on the table or the ground.

2. When you are in front of the tripod, your hands will be free to move, and your videos will be stable.

Source - Pixabay

Experts have said that your half body should be visible whenever you are making a video at least.

When you record a video from 6 to 7 minutes, make sure your hands are visible; this is possible only if you use the tripod.

CHAPTER EIGHTEEN

WHAT TO DO WITH YOUR VIDEO

Suppose you have recorded a video and you are thinking about what to do with the videos.

Let me share my experience here.

When I recorded the video for the first time, I took so many cuts in the middle to record a 2 minutes video.

If you take too many cuts in the middle of the video, then it will take extra time while edit that video.

So, I request you to record the video in one go, which will save you time and editing efforts.

The editing process is also time-consuming.

If you know editing work,,you can take cuts but try to avoid cuts as much as possible to save time.

To edit your videos, you can use movie maker or I-movie, inbuilt software on laptops.

If You want to edit your video on mobile, then you can use the VITA or Kinemaster App. (Free Version).

You can easily download it from the play store.

Five free and easy-to-use video editing software
Some of the software listed below are recommended for either Windows or Mac.
· Openshot
· Lightworks
· VSDC Video Editor
· Avidemux
· VideoPad
On YouTube, you can learn quickly about movie makers and I-movie.

You can search on YouTube for "How to use a movie maker in windows"?

First, try to focus on video, not editing.

Please don't try to add music, don't try to add video, and don't try to add subtitles with the first video.

Try to record the first video and enjoy it.

If you have taken cuts or splits while making video and thinking that what people will say, if there is a split,

or what people would say that you have taken so many retakes in the video.

Ok, to take cuts.

Don't worry about all this.

Don't even think about all this at the start.

Focus on your value and what you want to share with the world, not on these minor things.

There is no end to this.

Sometimes you fumble over the words but do not stop; you continue as long as you understand what you are saying.

You don't have to stop; it's not about being perfect; it's about being present and giving some value to people, which you have learnt in your life.

At the start, don't think about technical issues; you are not a professional YouTuber or someone expert.

Where To Upload Your Videos: - You can upload your video on the following platform.

1. Youtube

2. Linkedin

3. Facebook Page

(Sometimes, you can go live on social platforms. Sometimes you can make small reels, but do not waste time on small pieces of content. *Your content validity should be at least 5 to 10 years. Make videos for transforming the lives of people*)

Note: -

1. Don't run after likes, dislikes or subscribers.

2. At first, focus on YouTube because it's like the 2nd search engine after google.

3. If You are a sales expert, upload a video on both YouTube and LinkedIn.

4. Try to solve the problem of the people through your video.

5. Be consistent in making videos.

Conclusion

This book teaches you the mindset and skillset required to make videos.

Whenever I learn something, I always share it with the world. Now it's your turn to share with the world.

Some people plan to make videos once they become perfect, which is pretty impossible on this planet.

No one is perfect on this planet. Instead, just start making videos and gradually get flawless on your topic.

So, whenever you lose confidence, just focus on your target.

Remember, you have to make videos to help people and grow in your personal and professional life.

See,

You are not permanent on this planet.

You will not stay on this planet for 1000 years but for a limited time.

" You Must Record Video Before You Die"

So, don't leave this planet without making a single video.

Love & Respect,

Niraj Kumar Singh